U.S.A.

MEXICO

HAWAII IS.

Tokelau Is

Cook Is

Marquesas

SAMOA

Tuamotu Archipelago

Tonga

TAHITI

Rapa

Pitcairn

Easter Is

ZEALAND

HAWAII & POLYNESIA

Produced by James Siers
Designed by Peter Redstone
Edited by Lindsay Shelton
Type set in New Zealand

ISBN: 0-385-08167-7
Library of Congress Catalog Card Number 73-79878

Printed in Taipei, Taiwan by the
China Color Printing Co., Inc.

First published 1973

HAWAII & POLYNESIA
James Siers

DOUBLEDAY & COMPANY INC.
Garden City, New York

CONTENTS

6

ACKNOWLEDGEMENTS

My sincere thanks to all those who helped me, particularly to Shantilal Desai, Colin and Pat Weaver, Dan Costello, Tony Philp, and Claude Millar in Fiji; the Governor and Mrs Haydon, Tom and Chande Drabble, in American Samoa; Allan and Marina Grey and Tuala Paulo in Western Samoa; Bill and Mary Tiger and Les Enderton in Hawaii; Jean Lew and Gerard Gillateoux in Tahiti and Air New Zealand in the Pacific.

Vinaka Vaka Levu
Fa'afetai tele lava
Mahalo nui loa
Maururu roa

INTRODUCTION

Mention the words "Hawaii" or "Polynesia" in New York, or Paris on a cold winter's day and you'll get a sudden, fleeting breath of the warmth of the South Pacific. In the past, this vision had to remain a distant dream for most people. Today, in the age of jet travel, the dream is accessible.

The word *Polynesia* means *many islands*. Hawaii marks the northern-most limit of Polynesia. Easter Island marks the eastern corner of the great triangle and New Zealand in the south, more than 4,400 miles from Honolulu, establishes the boundaries of Polynesia.

This book should be titled "Polynesia." Yet, few of the visitors who come to Hawaii would associate the 50th State with the term. It might have been easier had the islands been called American Polynesia, much the same as the French call Tahiti and the Society Islands French Polynesia. Over the years Hawaii has established a unique flavour and character among the islands of the Pacific and it is in deference to its special place that this book acknowledges Hawaii in the title.

Hawaii became a State of the Union of the United States of America in 1959. The former territory achieved world prominence in 1942 when 200 Japanese aircraft attacked Pearl Harbor and various military installations on Oahu, bringing the United States into the war against Japan, Germany and Italy. This was the only attack. The subsequent military build-up for the war in the Pacific as well as a rapid post-war recovery, combined with Statehood in 1959, were the cause of an unprecedented economic boom. Today Hawaii welcomes more than a million tourists each year and Honolulu ranks as one of the vital cities of the United States.

The island group is the only one in Polynesia north of the equator. It is second only to New Zealand in land area, and second to none in scenic attractions.

Next to Hawaii, the islands of French Polynesia — with Tahiti as the focal point — owe more to myth and legend than all the other territories in the Pacific. Tahiti must always remain a special place. Not as spectacular as Hawaii yet somehow more beautiful; French since the 1840s, it remains Polynesian. Papeete still manages to retain the feeling of a small, pleasant town, with the added attraction of cafes which spill outdoors on to the sidewalk. You can sit there and watch the world go by.

A thousand miles to the west lie the islands of Western and American Samoa. Samoa is given the distinction of being the launching point of the great Polynesian movement to the East, and to this day it remains the most Polynesian of the islands in the group. Its traditional way of life has changed very little, especially in Western Samoa which is one of the smallest independent nations in the world.

Continuing south-west from Samoa, you come to the great archipelago of Fiji. The map will tell you this is outside the boundaries of Polynesia. The latest research, however, gives Fiji the distinction of being the birth-place of the Polynesian race. Perhaps of all the islands in the Pacific, Fiji has more to offer because of its diversity. It is the meeting place of east and west, not only from pre-historic times, but even now. It has more than 300 islands and some of the most attractive cruising water. Next to Hawaii it has the most cosmopolitan population. As well as the attractions of fine beaches, sheltered lagoons and tours at an economic price, it has some of the best duty-free shopping in the world. It is also the home of some of the friendliest people you can hope to find anywhere.

Fourteen-hundred miles south lies New Zealand. It is a fascinating blend of Maori people and British traditions; a deceptively large land: as big as Japan in land area, but with only three million people. It has a Western democracy and Western technology coupled with vast pasturelands; snowcapped mountains, trout streams, forests, geothermal areas and active volcanoes; more than sixty-million sheep and twenty-million cattle; more coastline than California and vast empty beaches, some of which like the 90-miles beach run beyond the point of sight.

This then is the scope of my book. A series of views of places and people which I hope suggest the individual character of each, while at the same time leaving an impression of the beauty, vitality and unique nature of the whole.

James Siers

HAWAII

American hoopla and Oriental industry; American know-how, Oriental application ... this is the theme of the progress of the 50th state of the Union. Much as the first settlers from the Marquesas gave way to the new migrants from Tahiti, so have the Hawaiians given way to the *haole* (whites) and the Chinese, Japanese, and Filippino migrants that the *haole* brought to work for him.

PRE-HISTORY

Hawaii was settled in two migrations. The first was from the Marquesas Islands. The second at a later date was from the Society Islands of French Polynesia, initially probably from Raiatea. This fact has now been established beyond dispute by the scientists of the Bernice P. Bishop Museum in Honolulu. The vital piece of evidence was a small stone disk, notched on one side and convex on another. Bishop Museum scientists recognised it as a game stone. Others have since been found in Hawaii and in the Society Islands, but nowhere else. In both Hawaii and the Society Islands (the leeward and windward islands of French Polynesia), the stones had gone out of use by the time of European discovery. Further evidence of Marquesan and Tahitian influence was found through the study of language, social-political structure and the comparison of artifacts.

When James Cook discovered Hawaii in 1778 and landed at Kauai, the people told him they had originally come from Kahiki (Tahiti). At that time the islands supported a large population of healthy, vigorous people. He traded with them before continuing his voyage to the northern coast of the American continent. His orders were to search for a north-west passage and to establish if possible a suggestion that a strait divided the continents of Europe and Asia from America. If this was proved, he was also to search for a north-east passage around the top of Russia.

Cook, with his two ships, the *Resolution* and the *Discovery,* spent the summer in executing the search and then in October 1778 returned to Hawaii to winter; to reprovision the ships with food and water and to overhaul the ships. He approached from the north-east and sighted the island of Maui. Then he cruised about the islands trading until January 1779 when he was off Kealakekua Bay on the big island of Hawaii. The anchorage proved suitable. The ships came in and anchored. By chance the English had stumbled on one of the greatest of Hawaiian festivals — the season of *Makahiki* — in honor of the god Lono. Hawaiian legend said that one day the god would return and Cook was acknowledged as the returning diety. The English were welcomed and treated with the utmost respect, though they began to suffer from a series of thefts which exasperated both sides until finally the Hawaiians grew weary and began to ask when the English would leave.

The *Resolution* and the *Adventure* sailed out of Kealakekua Bay on February the 4th. Almost immediately they were caught in a storm which damaged the foremast on the *Resolution*. The ships turned back and regained their anchorage on the 11th. On the 14th, Cook landed to take the principal chief, Kalaniopuu, hostage until the return of a ship's cutter which was stolen during the night. The Hawaiians opposed him. Cook shot a man, his marines fired, the Hawaiians charged. They killed Cook and five others and took away their bodies.

Peace was restored several days later. Some of the remains of Cook were returned and were buried at sea in accordance with English custom. The *Resolution* and the *Adventure* sailed away.

KAMEHAMEHA

A young chief named Kamehameha was at Kealakekua Bay when Cook was killed, and was injured by canon fire. He was destined to become the first king of the entire island group.

A civil war broke out on the death of Kalaniopuu (the chief whom Cook had intended to take hostage). The war lasted for nine years and was further complicated by a war with Maui. Kamehameha was appointed the keeper of the war god Kukailimoku. It was a fitting appointment by the dying Kalaniopuu, but it was to lead to the destruction of his own sons. Kamehameha destroyed the Maui force at the battle of the Iao Needle, returned to the island of Hawaii, tricked and killed his principal rival. He fought his final decisive battle on Oahu when he drove the defenders up the Nuuanu Valley, forcing many of the survivors to leap to their death from the *pali* (cliffs) at the end. In time the island of Kauai acknowledged his rule.

Kamehameha established a lasting peace, promulgated the law of the "splintered paddle" guaranteeing the rights of commoners and opened his country to trade with ships that came for sandalwood and whalers who came after sperm whales. He died in 1819 and was succeeded by his son, who took the title Kamehameha II.

MISSIONARIES

The missionaries arrived in Hawaii in 1820. They came from America and succeeded in overthrowing the Polynesian gods, and with them many of the restrictions. In place of these they substituted a strict set of christian laws which were considerably weakened by the fact that other Europeans who settled or called at Hawaii during this time, though also Christian, did not bother to keep.

Combined with their good work in teaching the people to read and write in their own language and in teaching them trades and crafts, the missionaries also established their families as prominent landholders. Their descendants to this day are sometimes the butt of a Hawaiian joke which goes something like this: "Before the missionary came, the Hawaiian lay on the beach in the sun and enjoyed the good things of life without excessive labor. Now the Hawaiian labors while the sons of the missionaries lie on the beach in the sun." The observation is obviously superficial. The whole is the subject of a much wider controversy.

EUROPEAN INFLUENCE

In 1794 the British took possession of the islands in the name of the King. But Britain did not acknowledge the possession made on its behalf by Captain Vancouver. Vancouver was one of the ensigns who sailed with Cook on his last voyage. In retrospect, it might have been better for the Hawaiians if Britain had taken possession and guaranteed Hawaiian ownership of land. The growing and harvesting of sugar cane for the production of sugar was to develop into a major industry. It was to be the key factor in Hawaii's annexation by the United States. The market for the sugar was on the mainland. But as long as Hawaii remained an independent nation it was subject to restrictive tariff laws at the whim of Congress.

The need for labor for the plantations was also responsible for today's cosmopolitan population. Indentured labor was brought in from China, Japan, Portugal, Scandanavia and the Philippines.

THE REPUBLIC

The seventh heir to the throne of Kamehameha was Princess Liliuokalani. She came to power in 1891 and was deposed in 1893 when Hawaii was proclaimed a republic. An attempt to restore her to power by a armed *coup* failed in 1894. The *coup* was used as a pretext to force her to sign an unconditional renounciation of the throne. Four years later Hawaii became a territory of the United States. In 1959 it became the 50th State of the Union.

HAWAII TODAY

Hawaii today enjoys a booming economy based on its sugar industry, the pineapple industry which is the biggest in the world, the tourist industry and the military presence. Total income from all external sources would amount to more than $1000,000,000 yearly. But Hawaii is not a place which may be measured by facts and figures, however impressive. It is America's western-most state where the saying of another generation is valid today: Go west young man, the *Aloha* state is waiting for you.

TAHITI

Tahiti is as much a state of mind as it is a place in the South Pacific. It symbolises more than any other island the total myth of the South Sea legend. Tahiti was the first major discovery in east Polynesia at a time when the concept of the "noble savage" was at its height in Europe. The sailors from the British man-o-war, *H.M.S. Dolphin,* which is credited with the discovery in 1767, and the men of Bougainville's ship, which called the following year, brought back stories of a sub-tropical paradise where it was never cold, no one went hungry, and where lovemaking was free of stigma.

To a cold, weary, war-torn Europe, this was a romantic picture. Yet, though it was true as far as it went, it was also misleading. The Tahitians had opposed Captain Wallis of the *Dolphin,* and he killed many of them before he could land. Tahiti was a land of abundance, but for some it was possible to starve; the Tahitians were unabashed about love-making, but in accordance with social rank and custom. The noble savage also had some savage notions about the equality of men. The bulk of the population was held in serfdom by hereditary chiefs in almost the same way that peasants were held in Europe, with the added disadvantage of not knowing when they might be chosen as human sacrifice to be offered to the gods.

Tahiti is the centre of a large group of islands. The islands were annexed by France and are now known as French Polynesia. This definition includes the islands of Tahiti, Moorea, Mehetia, Tetiaroa, Maiao (known as the windward islands) and those to the leeward: Huahine, Raiatea-Tahaa, and Bora Bora. It also includes the Tuamotu atolls, the Austral Islands, Gambier Islands, Marquesas and the Rapa Islands.

At the time of European discovery, Tahiti had established itself as the most powerful and populous island of the group. It had surpassed Raiatea, which is now being acknowledged as the former political and religious centre of East Polynesia. Tahitian navigator-priests had sailed to discover Hawaii, the Cook Islands and New Zealand. They maintained sea contact with Samoa and the Tuamotus. They were an open, candid, physically attractive people who made men such as Captain James Cook wonder at their versatility and added to the puzzle of their origin.

The Tahitians are Polynesian. Their immediate previous home was most likely Samoa. The islands of Savaii and Upolu (Tahitian "h" for "S" and "r" for "l") in Samoa have their counterpart in Raiatea, formerly Hawaii and Tahaa, formerly Uporu. They were settled possibly as early as 200 B.C.-

during a golden age of Polynesian movement around the Pacific and as the population built up, spread over the windward group.

When Wallis sailed into Matavai Bay in 1767, Tahiti had a large population under the rule of several chiefs one of whom was eventually to establish paramount title. The man took the name of Pomare and began the conquest which was consolidated by his son. It was during his son's reign, which began in 1803, that the most significant events occurred in Tahiti. His father had welcomed missionaries in 1797. Pomare II saw the Christian faith extended, though he himself subscribed to it in an odd way: by conducting an incestuous affair with his two sisters and by prodigious drinking, which sent him to an early grave. His young son (Pomare III) quickly followed him to the grave and the kingdom passed to Pomare's 15-year-old daughter Aimata. It was her unhappy fate to see it pass to the French. Her hopes of British intervention were never realised. She died in 1877 after a reign of 50 years. Her son, who took the title of Pomare V, formally signed over his kingdom to France three years later.

MISSIONARIES

Following the discovery of Tahiti by Wallis and Bougainville, the great British navigator and explorer, James Cook, used the island in 1769 as a base for scientific investigation and exploration. He called there on two subsequent voyages. The last was to lead to the discovery of Hawaii in 1778, and to Cook's death at Kealakekua Bay on the island of Hawaii in 1779. The sailing master of Cook's command ship the *Resolution* on that fateful voyage was a 22-year-old officer named William Bligh, whose later command of *H.M.S. Bounty* and its mutiny is one of the better known stories of Tahiti.

The first Europeans to settle in Tahiti were evangelists from the London Missionary Society. This was the first attempt to bring the word of god to the South Seas. It was made in 1797 when the society's ship *Duff* arrived at Matavai Bay. The Tahitians were reluctant converts; the mission languished and nearly closed in 1809. In 1815 Pomare II lent his support and from that point the population quickly accepted the new faith.

French interest in Tahiti dates from the voyage of Bougainville. But it was not until 1836, when two French Catholic priests were turned away, that events were set in motion which finally resulted in the cession of the island to France.

MUTINY ON THE BOUNTY

The British were a commercial nation and it was a commercial interest which was responsible for the dispatch of Lieutenant William Bligh in *H.M.S. Bounty* to Tahiti in 1787. The 22-year-old sailing master was now 31. Despite favourable mention by Cook during his last voyage, this was Bligh's first command. The British had possessions in the Caribbean. Some of them, such as Jamaica, produced sugar cane and rum. The work was done by slaves.. Slaves had to be fed Might not the profits be better if the food was cheaper? The logic was irrefutable. If breadfruit thrived in the Pacific it would surely thrive in the Caribbean. If it produced healthy, strong people in Polynesia, might it not do the same elsewhere?

Among the eager crew, Bligh selected a former shipmate and friend, Fletcher Christian, made him an officer and set sail. The voyage had the usual irritations, and was made worse by the suspicion that Bligh had diverted some of the ship's provisions to his home before the ship left England. He arrived in Tahiti in the wrong season, when the breadfruit plants could not be potted, and left six months later with his cargo.

The mutiny began on the morning of April 28, 1789, off one of the islands in Tonga. Christian Fletcher took possession of the *Bounty* and put Bligh and 18 others who were loyal to him in the ship's launch, gave them some food, water, four cutlasses and a sextant and cut him adrift. He remained deaf to Bligh's plea as to what would happen to his (Bligh's) wife and children. Except for one man who was killed in a skirmish with Tongans, Bligh brought the others safely to Java more than 3,500 miles away. He lived to distinguish himself and to personally receive commendation from Nelson at the battle of Copenhagen in 1801. But despite his courage and devotion to duty, Bligh continued to have public relations problems. He suffered two more mutinies during his long career.

Most of the mutineers were re-captured in Tahiti, but Christian and seven others were never found. They settled on Pitcairn's Island in the remote South East corner of Polynesia with Tahitian wives and some Tahitian men. The Tahitians, who found themselves regarded as second-rate citizens of the tiny island, mutinied and killed four Englishmen, including Christian. The remaining English with the help of their Tahitian wives, in turn killed all the Tahitian men. Three of the remaining mutineers died violent deaths. When the American whaler *Topaz* re-discovered the island in 1808, only one man was left. He was John Adams, surrounded by the Tahitian women and the-offspring of the mutineers, finally solved the mystery of the what happened to Christian after the mutiny on the *Bounty*.

ART IN TAHITI

Perhaps it is because of the French attitude to life, or perhaps it is because of a fashion started by Paul Gaugain, that Tahiti today supports a number of first-rate artists. What is more it supports them a good deal better than it supported the master himself. Gaugain left a legacy worth millions of dollars today, while in his own time he often went hungry. He lived in Tahiti twice and finally removed himself to the Marquesas islands where he died of syphillis.

Among the artists living in French Polynesia today are Jean Masson, at Bora Bora, and his friend Francois Ravello, who lives at Moorea. Both have distinguished themselves. An example of their work is featured in the color plates on Tahiti. Masson spent 18 years in the stark, austere Tuamotu atolls. When he returned to live permanently in Tahiti, his friend Ravello, for a time shared his *fare* at Point Venus.

TAHITI TODAY

Two events within the past decade have transformed the island of Tahiti from a languid South Sea island to a busy, bustling center of French Polynesia: the international airport at Faaa and the French nuclear testing programme at Mururoa. Papeete has been transformed, the harbor changed beyond recognition, the roads sealed and in the flow of cash that accompanied the French Navy, the attitude of the people suddenly changed. A flood of tourists has swept in to see for themselves where it all happened. Luxurious hotels have gone up to cater for their demands. As well as luxury, French Polynesia offers what no other territory or nation can offer: Polynesian people and a French way of life mixed in a heady cocktail with myth, legend and incredible beauty.

SAMOA

Part of the attraction of Polynesia is its diversity. Each of the five territories in this book is related and yet distinct. A stream of related themes binds the whole. Each of the island groups is of volcanic origin. Therefore the great peaks and cliffs of Hawaii have their counterpart in Samoa, Tahiti, Fiji and New Zealand. The *fires of Maui* (active volcanoes) burn with their crimson flame and sulphur fumes in Hawaii, Samoa and New Zealand. The native peoples are of the same origin with related cultures, customs and language and yet each is different.

Of all the differences, Samoa is *more* different. It is, as the tourist office says, the best-kept secret of the South Pacific. If you want to know how the Hawaiians lived a hundred years ago, you will get a good idea in Samoa. It is still a land where status is more important than material possessions and the only Polynesian culture where the title is more important than the person. Whereas the hereditary succession marked chiefs in other parts of Polynesia, in Samoa any member of the family may succeed to the principal title.

The great colonial grab by Western powers during the last century saw the islands divided between Imperial Germany and the United States. In 1962 Western Samoa became independent but Tutuila and the islands of Manua remain an American territory administered by the Department of the Interior.

PRE-HISTORY

The islands of Samoa were settled before 300 B.C. The first settlement could have been as early as 1000 B.C. The first settlers arrived from Tonga via Fiji in the great dispersal of the Polynesian race. From here they launched their double canoes to the east to Tahiti, the Marquesas, the Cook islands and eventually from there to all the other island groups of the Eastern Pacific. The discovery and settlement of Samoa from the northern islands of Tonga would have been relatively easy as the distance is only approximately a hundred miles. The Tongans had established a thriving central form of Government which required frequent canoe voyaging between their various islands. For a period, no doubt, the islands of Samoa would have been subject to Tonga. Eventually they won independence although they were later to lose it again to the Tongans. Today's Head of State of Western Samoa, Malietoa Tanumafili II, is the bearer of the *Malietoa* title relating to the second expulsion of the Tongans from Samoa. The departing Tongan chief gave him the title after his force had been swept up by the Samoan army. As the Tongan canoes got under way their chief shouted to his Samoan counterpart:

"Malietoa, Malietu!" — Brave warrior, well fought.

The leader of the Samoan army assumed the title and in time it became one of four great Samoan titles which ruled the islands of Western and American Samoa. The 5th important title was that of the Tui Manua (King of Manua) which lapsed with the death of the last king of Manua. He had willed that his title should be discontinued when his islands were taken over by the United States in 1900.

The Dutch, who with the Spanish, were active in the Pacific from an early date are given the credit of having discovered the Samoan group. Jacob Roggeveen sighted the group during his circumnavigation of the world in 1721-1722. He did not land. The Frenchman La Perouse called next in 1787. Twelve men including the commandant of one of the two ships, were killed during a landing for water at Asu on the island of Tutuila in American Samoa.

Europeans left the islands alone until the early 1800s. Economic opportunity drew the adventurer. The usual pattern was to establish a trading post and sell the natives grog and guns in return for copra, turtle shell and artifacts. Some of the Europeans attached themselves as mercenaries to the leading families. The introduction of guns and the disruption of the balance of power led to a series of brutal wars. It was a pattern repeated in all the other island groups of Polynesia. In Samoa the support of Europeans first led some of the leading families to a paramount position.

In 1830 John Williams of the London Missionary Society landed in Savaii in a schooner he had built in the Cook Islands. He had christened his ship the *Messenger of Peace* but despite the ready acceptance of the new faith by the Samoans, there was to be no peace. His landfall co-incided with the assumption of power by the Malietoa family. It was made possible by the assassination of a despotic ruler named Tamafaiga who had combined the offices of chief and high priest within his person. Tamafaiga's death created a vacuum eagerly filled by Williams with the blessing of Malietoa. To this day the faith propagated by Williams remains the principal denomination and although no longer controlled from London is still known as L.M.S.

As elsewhere in the Pacific, the Samoan language was first converted to writing by missionaries. In this case it was a man named Charles Braff who came to Samoa with Williams. By the 1840s Samoan missionaries were leaving their homeland to take the word of god to the people of Niue, the Tokelaus, the Gilbert and Ellice Islands and to the New Hebrides.

At this time the great European powers were beginning to annex and colonise islands in the Pacific. New Zealand was ceded to Britain in 1840; the island of Tahiti was under virtual French control; Australia was a British possession; Imperial Germany was already making plans for an active role in the Pacific; the Spanish had the Philippines and the Dutch Java. There was little hope that small states such as Samoa could maintain political independence.

The rivalry for Samoa was a three-way affair between Germany, Britain and the United States. German interests were established in 1856 with the establishment of the trading firm of Cesar Godeffroy und Sohn, of Hamburg. The company was already active in Chile and the Tuamotus. After opening the Samoa branch, it quickly expanded into Fiji and Tonga. Within a few years the firm had a network of branches in Niue, Futuna, Wallis Island, the Tokelaus, the Gilbert and Ellice Islands, the Northern Solomons, New Hebrides, New Britain, New Ireland and Nauru. Along with the Caroline and Marshall islands, many of these territories eventually became German possessions.

Each of the powers took the side of a prominent family and pressed its claims to the supreme title with the objective quite clear: divide and rule and finally take possession. The worst meddling was by the consuls of the three nations. A series of wars was the result until 1873, when the last battle was fought around Apia. In 1889 a treaty between the three powers guaranteed Samoa's independence, but nine years later in Berlin it was agreed that Germany should take over Western Samoa and the United States should take Tutuila and the islands of Manua. Britain waived her right to Savaii in return for German acknowledgement of Britain's right to Tonga.

During the height of the final confrontation between the three powers in 1889, there were seven warships in the Apia roadstead; three German, three American and one British. Just at the point when a new war was imminent and naval intervention, seemed likely, a hurricane swept in. Only the British ship escaped. Today as you stand on the reclamation in the harbour you can imagine what happened as the doomed ships were driven on the reef and broken. Even as the German and American ships were giving way, the British, with superb skill, slowly gained for the open sea. They passed the Trenton and the American sailors cheered her on. The Germans lost 92 men, the Americans 54.

Today, past troubles seem long forgotten, but the memory of one man, who lived in Apia during those troubled times, is very much alive. The man was Robert Louis Stevenson, a writer of stirring adventure stories whom the Samoans fondly referred to as *Tusitala* (the storyteller). It seems strange that while Apia makes much of the fact that Stevenson lived there, it was another writer, who put Pago Pago on the map. The man was Somerset Maugham and the story was "Rain."

Stevenson came to Samoa in search of better health. He had tuberculosis and in retrospect it seems unusual that he sought the wet, humid climate of Samoa. He built a modest cottage at Vailima up the hill three miles from the waterfront. In his wife's diary there is reference to the fact that he felt his health had improved in Samoa. Nevertheless he died in 1894 only four years after his arrival. His grave lies on top of Mount Vaea some 500 feet above Vailima, which is now greatly expanded and the official residence of the Head of State.

In 1914 at the start of the First World War, New Zealand troops took possession of Western Samoa on behalf of Britain. In 1962 the islands became an independent state.

American Samoa still remains a territory of the United States.

Apia today is much the same as it has been for fifty years, though some of the famous landmarks, such as the Casino Hotel built for the German administration have disappeared.

In Pago Pago, there has been a good deal of change in the past ten years. An international airport was built at Tafuna. For those who have been here it must surely rate as one of the most pleasant and attractive in the world. There are several new hotels; a new auditorium; new roading; a water supply; an electricity supply and with the arrival of the new Governor, John M. Haydon in 1969, new prospects for greater political power to the Samoan people.

Those who visit Samoa (both Western and American) cannot help but be impressed by the courtesy of the people and the restful, low-key atmosphere. The islands retain a charm which will continue to lure those in search of the past. But as the word gets around Samoa won't be the "best kept secret of the South Pacific" any more.

FIJI

Fiji has the unusual distinction of being the birth-place of the Polynesian race. Carbon dating has established occupation in Fiji as early as 1500 B.C. This fact alone has shattered many of concepts about the movement of people in the South Pacific. The latest theory, proposed by Dr. Kenneth Emory of the Bishop Museum in Hawaii, is that there was no such thing as a Polynesian race before the settlement of Fiji. Various ethnic groups who made their way to these islands were able to develop from hereditary genes and through inter-marriage, into a distinct physical type.

How great a role the Melanesian Negritoid people played in this development is not known but the inter-action continued until European discovery of the island groups. What is certain, however, is that the Polynesians eventually lost their original home and moved east to Tonga.

Fijians are physically impressive. The men are tall and well-built; bigger than the Melanesian peoples of New Caledonia, the New Hebrides and the Solomons. The legends of the early navigators speak of them with awe as uncompromising cannibals whose taste for human flesh rivalled that of the Maori of New Zealand and the fierce warriors of the Marquesas islands. They were skilled sailors and maintained contact with Tonga and Samoa where they were frequently used as mercenaries. Samoan legends constantly refer to Fiji and speak of Fijian raiders who subjugated part of their islands in the dawn of their history.

At the time of European discovery, the islands were ruled by several powerful chiefs. The state of Rewa, near Suva, was most powerful. With the help of European mercenaries, the small island of Bau quickly rose to prominence. As elsewhere, the introduction of guns precipitated a series of devastating wars. The power of firearms was first demonstrated by Charles Savage. He was a survivor of the wrecked ship *Eliza* in 1805. He made his way to Bau, which at that time was at war with Rewa. A canoe took him up the Rewa River and drew up near one of the fortified villages. Standing on a platform so that he could easily see into the village, Savage began to shoot the defenceless inhabitants. After he had shot a large number, the survivors piled up the bodies and hid behind the corpses of their friends and relatives.

Sandalwood first induced Europeans to move into the reef-infested waters. Huge profits awaited those who were daring enough. They were followed by other adventurers whose main interest was to wrest away the power of the Fijians and to acquire as much land as possible. British settlers began to move up from the springboard of the Australian and New Zealand colonies. There were some Americans, too. The Tongans, under a powerful chief, Maafu, were entranched in the Lau islands. In the wars and disputes which followed up to the time of cession of Fiji to Britain in 1874, Tongans held the balance of power.

The men of destiny of the time was the Bauan Chief, Seru Cakobau, who extended the power of his state to the point where he was able to call himself Tui Viti (King of Fiji). He was principal in the offer of cession. British rule of the islands ended in 1970 when Fiji became an independent nation within the British Commonwealth. The descendants of Cakobau have maintained their position as leaders of the community.

Copra and *bech de mer* replaced sandalwood. An American began to press sugar cane to make sugar. During the American Civil War the flats of Navua were planted in cotton. The Fijians were not subservient laborers and the islands became part of the "blackbirding" trade. This was nothing short of a slave trade, masked by the name of "contract" labor. In effect men from the New Hebrides were tricked about such "contracts" and found themselves sold into bondage. The Deed of Cession put a final end to "blackbird" labor in Fiji.

At this time, sugar cane growing and milling was assuming an important role in the economy of the new colony. To meet the labor requirements of this industry indentured labor was brought out from India in 1879. A series of shipments brought men to work in the plantations until the practice was stopped in 1916. In that year there were 60,000 Indians in Fiji, many of them born in the colony. 40,000 decided to remain in Fiji and today their progeny account for more than half of the total population of all races which numbers approximately half a million people.

British possession of the islands guaranteed Fijian ownership of land. Today the Fijians own 83 per cent of all the land in the country. This has meant that the descendants of the Indians have had to turn to other fields for their economic development. Many are tenant farmers on Fijian land; they are the businessmen in the towns and store owners in the country-side; the professional people: lawyers, doctors, nurses, dentists, accountants; they are the tradesmen, cartage contractors and primary producers.

This is one of the features that makes Fiji an outstanding visitor attraction — it offers such a wide choice of things to do and places to see. There are more than 300 islands in the group. Up to 150 of these are inhabited. Many of these lie within sheltered water and offer superb cruising. Take the Nadi-Lautoka area as an example. To the west lies the Mamanuca chain with superb beaches and almost constant sunshine. On the way you pass small gems of islands such as Danny Costello's *Beachcomber.* To the north the Yasawas stretch in a necklace of green and turquoise over the deep blue of the Pacific. On your way there you pass Colin Weaver's Vomo Island.

Captain William Bligh passed through here in 1789 after losing his ship, *H.M.S. Bounty,* to Fletcher Christian and other mutineers off Tonga. His epic voyage in an open boat with 17 others remains an outstanding feat of known navigation. It was while passing through the Vatu-I-Ra channel between Viti Levu and Vanua Levu that his voyage was almost cut short. A large Fijian double canoe put out in pursuit and managed to come within bow-shot of Bligh and his men. A Fijian chief fired several arrows, none of which hit their mark, and abandoned the chase when the wind dropped, leaving Bligh to sail the rest of the 3,500 miles to Java.

Next to Samoa, Fiji gives the impression of having retained most of its ancient customs and rituals. *Kava,* which is known in Fiji as *yaqona* is still taken both socially and during important occasions. The practice of the presentation of the *tabua* (a sperm whale's tooth) is very much a prerequisite today to social and business obligations. Fijians love to sing and dance and have maintained their colorful *mekes.* In olden days these were perhaps more varied than today. There were fierce war dances by the men; humorous story ballets and gentle dances by the women. Today they are still part of Fijian culture and may be seen to advantage during the annual independence celebrations, at festivals or during the installations of high chiefs.

No reference to Fiji would be complete without a mention of the extreme cannibalism practised here in the days before cession. It was part of everyday life. People beaten in war were derisively called "food for the pot." A chief at Rakiraki was said to have eaten 900 men (though this sounds like an exaggeration); Europeans witnessed cannibal feasts where many bodies were cut up and cooked in earth ovens. One of the largest such feasts took place on the island of Bau after the taking of Verata in 1839. The bodies of 260 men, women and children were eaten.

The English poet Rupert Brooke visited Fiji in 1913. He found past cannibalism hard to reconcile with the extreme friendliness of the people and he wrote a humorous piece in a note home:

The limbs that erstwhile charmed your sight
   Are now a savage's delight;
The ear that heard your whispered vow
   Is one of many entrees now;
Broiled are the arms in which you clung,

And devilled is the angelic tongue: . . .
And oh! my anguish as I see
A black man gnaw your favourite knee;
Of the two eyes that were your ruin,
One now observes the other stewing.
My lips (the inconstancy of man!)
Are yours no more. The legs that ran
Each dewy morn their love to wake,
Are now a steak, are now a steak!

And as another man of another generation might have said: and so we bid
fond farewell to the lovely land of Isa Lei.

NEW ZEALAND

New Zealand is an independent nation within the British Commonwealth. It has the same political status as Canada and Australia. It is still also very much Polynesia. Auckland, the largest city, is also the biggest Polynesian city in the world. New Zealand has the largest Polynesian population in the Pacific. As well as the Maori people, there are Samoans, Cook Islanders, Niue Islanders, Tokelauans and a small number of Tongans.

Because of the small total population — New Zealand has only 3,000,000 people in a land area greater than California and as great as Japan's where there are 100,000,000 people — and a low political profile, it is known only to a few discriminating travellers and those with an interest in world geography.

PRE-HISTORY

Polynesian navigators discovered the islands (on present carbon dates of occupation sites) in approximately 500 A.D. This date may not be early enough. Only a continuing effort in field work is likely to uncover additional evidence. Maori traditions speak of several distinct settlement periods culminating in a fleet of seven canoes from Hawaiki (Tahitian Havai'i or Raiatea) in about 1300 A.D. Scholars regard the fleet theory with suspicion and there's been some suggestion that it may refer to a movement south from New Zealand's Bay of Islands following a population build-up. The Polynesian demi-god Maui is given the credit of raising New Zealand from the sea. Legend says that he pursued a great fish and finally caught and brought it to the surface where it became the North Island of New Zealand.

The first settlers found a vast land with a mild climate and huge economic resources. At that time New Zealand was the home of several rare and unique bird species, the largest of which was the great moa. The land was covered by bush and grassland and areas of fertile soil where the sweet potato, the *kumara,* would thrive. The coastline teemed with fish and shellfish. The lakes and rivers were stocked with fish and waterfowl. The first part of Maori settlement and occupation is now referred to as the moa-hunter period. The population was small and migratory, moving in pursuit of the large birds. As the population built-up and the moa was exterminated, there was a permanent settlement of the warmer, fertile areas of northern New Zealand followed by a gradual permanent settlement of most of the country by tribes and sub-tribes. The population was greatest in the areas where it was easiest to grow the *kumara*. Disputes over land led to war and the classical period of Maori culture began. The classic Maori culture is marked by several distinct features: the development of cannibalism, the development of a highly-refined material culture, the expression of which is found today in surviving lavish and intricate wood carving, facial and body tattoo; canoe building; weaving; the working of New Zealand jade into cutting tools such as adzes, weapons such as short clubs and into personal ornaments such as ear pendants and *hei tikis*.

Two navigators first associated with the discovery of New Zealand, Abel Tasman in 1643 and James Cook in 1769, both lost men to the cannibal Maoris. Tasman's shock at seeing his men killed made him leave New Zealand without an attempt at landing.

James Cook first came to New Zealand to investigate the Dutchman's discovery and to find out whether it was part of a great southern continent. He established New Zealand as a group of islands and returned again in 1772-1775 to use the islands as a base for the exploration of the southern South Pacific and the subsequent voyages to Antarctica. During the course of this voyage, five of his men were killed and cut up for a cannibal feast by the Maoris.

As in Tahiti and Hawaii, which lay on the migration path of the sperm whale, New Zealand became important to whalers. Shore stations were established and each year there was the usual influx of whaling ships. The whalers traded guns and grog for food and women and contributed to local wars. Guns made greater wars possible and combined with new diseases, to which the native people had no immunity, reduced the local population. These were bad omens for the Maori. The missionaries followed and in their wake, land-hungry settlers. The settlers in turn pressed for protection and in 1840, following a series of negotiations and coercion, principal Maori chiefs convened at Waitangi in the Bay of Islands to sign a document of cession. The British flag was raised. A salute was fired and shiploads of new settlers began to leave Britain. New Zealand was settled at about the same time that the movement of Europeans began from the eastern States of America to the west with the same confrontation between the holders of the land, and their own desire for it. In New Zealand, one of the clauses of the treaty of cession signed at Waitangi, was the guarantee of fair land dealing. Disputes arising out of this question and the Maori awareness that his race was in danger, led to a series of wars, the worst of which took part in the center of the North Island from the 1860's to the 1870's. The result of the wars was a defeat of the Maori and the confiscation of a great deal of his land which is an issue even to this day.

There are, however, still large areas of Maori land in New Zealand and the people enjoy equal status and opportunity in the eyes of the law. In practical terms the Maori has not been able to compete with the European except in a minority of cases. There is no overt discrimination and a good deal of integration and inter-marriage. There is also a growing public awareness that more must be done to allow the Maori people of New Zealand to assume equal status in real terms.

DEVELOPMENT

The country developed through the export of agricultural products until gold was discovered in the South Island in the 1860s. This led to a large influx of miners, many of whom chose to remain in the country. The introduction of refrigeration made it possible to export butter and meat to Europe and led to further development of the country. The bush which once covered most of New Zealand was burnt off and replaced by pasture so that today the country gives the impression that it is in fact a vast pastureland. The economy is still 80 per cent dependent on agriculture; principally on meat, wool and dairy products. To produce goods for export, New Zealand farmers raise more than 60 million sheep; more than 20 million beef and dairy cattle.

In the 1930's New Zealand led the world in social legislation with the introduction of free medical services, free education and a social security system which also provided a retirement pension. Both Maori and *pakeha* (whites) joined to fight against Imperial Germany during the Great War and again in the Second World War in 1939-45. The battles of Midway and Coral Sea won by America following Japan's entry into the war with the bombing of Honolulu, saved New Zealand from a Japanese invasion.

In the years since the Second World War, New Zealand has expanded its economy. Although agriculture still accounts for most of the exports, timber and manufactured goods are now important in the earning of overseas exchange. Britain's entry into the European Common Market will eventually lead to a greater dependence by New Zealand on the Pacific basin.

SCENIC

Scenically New Zealand is described as a wonderland. It has everything which appeals to the visitor: snow-capped mountains which offer excellent skiing; beautiful lakes and rivers full of trout; uncrowded beaches and friendly, hospitable people. Among the outstanding visitor attractions are the thermal areas of Rotorua-Taupo and the Mount Cook, Queenstown and Milford Sound areas of the South Island.

Hawaii: *opposite,* a Hawaiian girl. *Overleaf,* an eruption in 1972 at the Volcanoes National Park, Island of Hawaii.

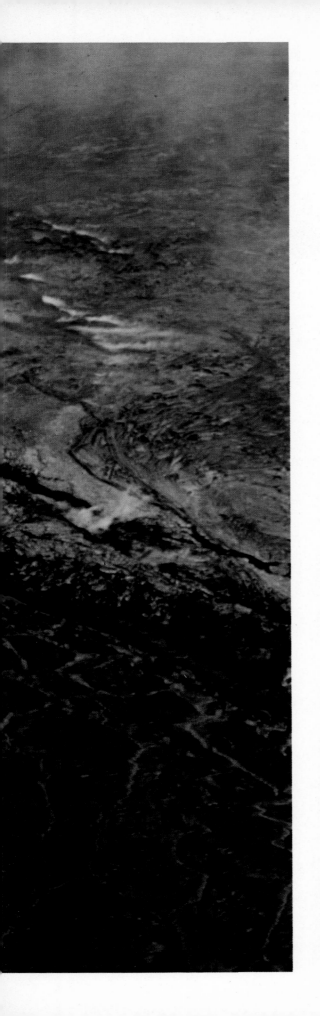

32

Below, a body surfer about to be dumped Makaha, Oahu.
Opposite, storm surf and surfer Honolua Bay, Maui.

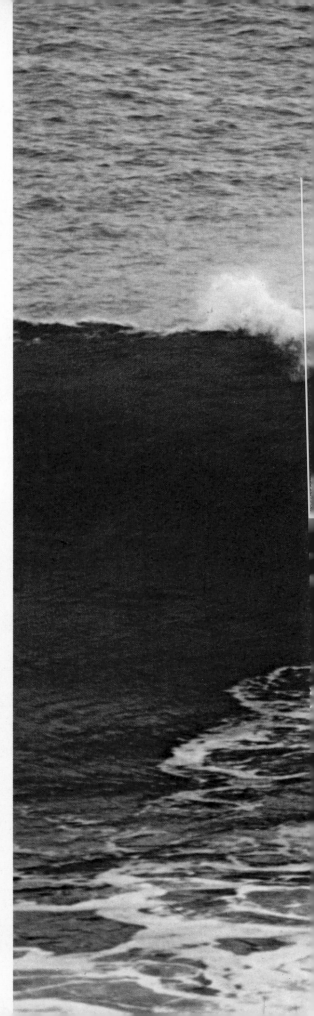

Left, Waikiki Beach, Honolulu. *Below*, girl watching, Waikiki. *Overleaf*, Mauna Kea snow fields, Island of Hawaii.

40

Sea Life Park, Makapuu, Oahu, *Overleaf,* Haleakala Crater, Maui.

44

Below, Makawao, ranch country, Maui. *Opposite,* Waimea,
Hawaii. *Overleaf,* the beautiful beach at Hanalei Bay,
Kauai.

Kalalau Valley, Kauai.

TAHITI

Early navigators considered the women of Tahiti the most beautiful in the Pacific. *Overleaf*, Hotel Bora Bora and the lagoon and reef, Island of Bora Bora.

Papetoai Bay, Moorea.

Children of Tahiti.

60

Taharaa black sand beach, Tahiti. *Overleaf,* another view from the same position — looking towards Papeete and Moorea.

Below, fishermen, Raiatea. *Opposite* the work of Francois Ravello, *left,* and Jean Masson. *Below left,* Ravello sits near a "no-stop" sign in a characteristic disregard for the conventional attitude. He lives in Moorea and Jean Masson, in Bora Bora.

66

Papenoo River and Valley, Tahiti.

68

Lagoon and Pirogue, Bora Bora.

Below, church, Tiarei, Tahiti.
Opposite, sunset from Hotel
Oa Oa, near Vaitape, Bora Bora

SAMOA

Below, fautasi, Apia Harbor. *Opposite,* Pago Pago from the
summit of Mt Pioa (The Rainmaker).

Opposite, "Two Dollar Beach", American Samoa and *below*, the Congregationalist Church at Leone, American Samoa, with a memorial to the Rev. John Williams who brought Christianity to Samoa.
Overleaf, left, dancer at Aggies Hotel, Apia. *Right, kava* ceremony Manua, American Samoa. *Centre*, tattooing, Lefaga, Western Samoa.

78

Hotel Pago Pago, American
Samoa. *Overleaf,* football
American Samoan style.

Women of Samoa. *Overleaf,* left, the dance of the *Taupou,* Western Samoa. *Right,* Dr Margaret Mead, whose book "The Coming of Age in Samoa" made her famous dances a *siva* on her return to Manua, American Samoa.

Bonito boat off Foalalo, Savaii, Western Samoa.

90

The extraordinary island of Apolima, Western Samoa, has a village inside the volcanic cone and only one landing place. *Opposite,* Air New Zealand jet at Tafuna, American Samoa. This must be one of the most delightful international airports in the world.

FIJI

Below, young girls in Suva's "liquid sunshine." *Left*, children, upper Sigatoka River Valley. *Overleaf*, diver and fish, Astrolabe Lagoon, Kadavu. *Right*. young fishermen and catch, upper Sigatoka River.

Women of Fiji. *Overleaf,* the lagoon at
Nabukeru, Island of Yasawa

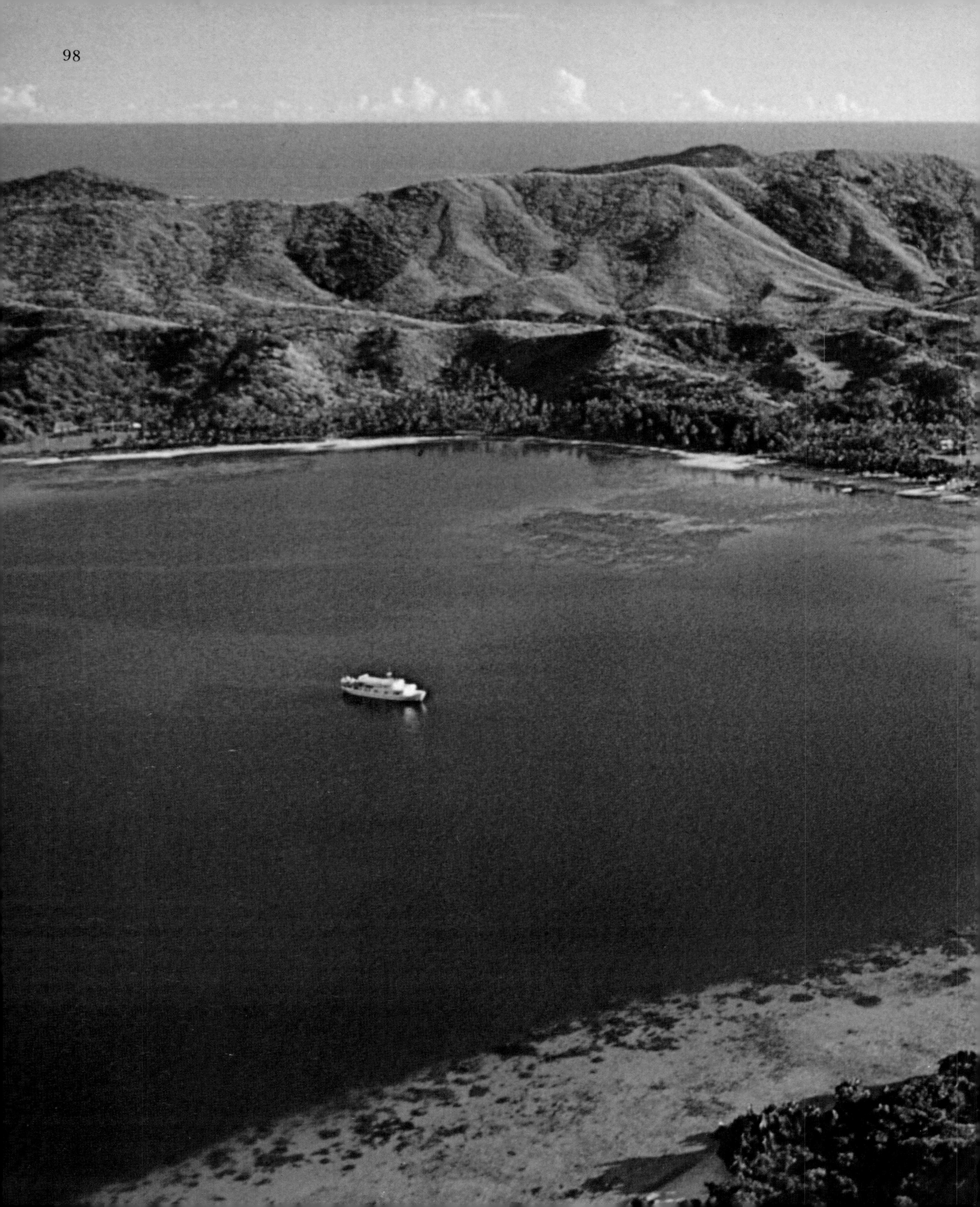

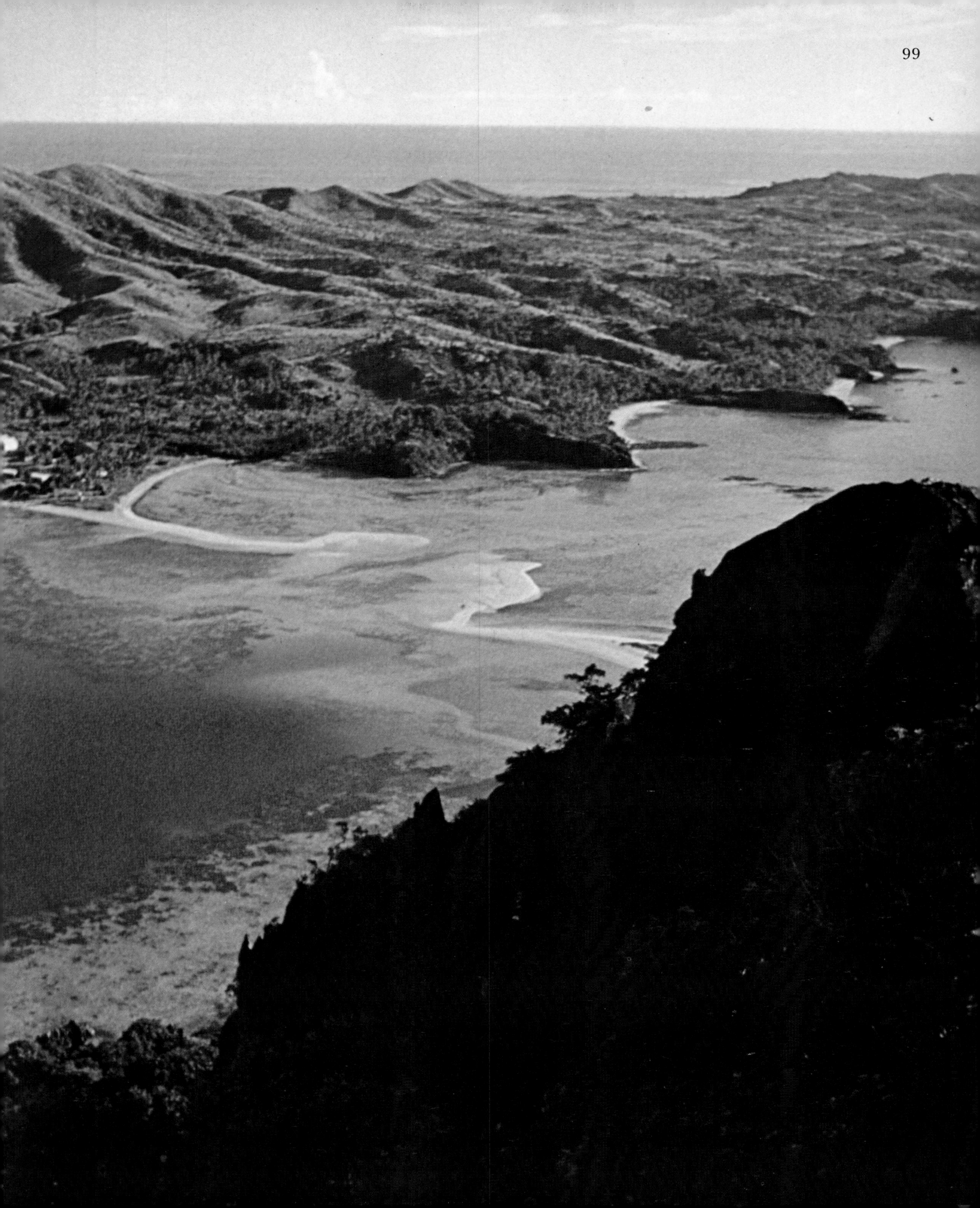

Sayandra in the Astrolabe Lagoon, Kadavu.

Nandi flats with the Sambeto River in the foreground

Vomo Island, Bligh Water.

Meke! Left, the Orchid Island group, Suva. *Right*, a member of the Kabu Kei Vuda, Viseisei, Lautoka.

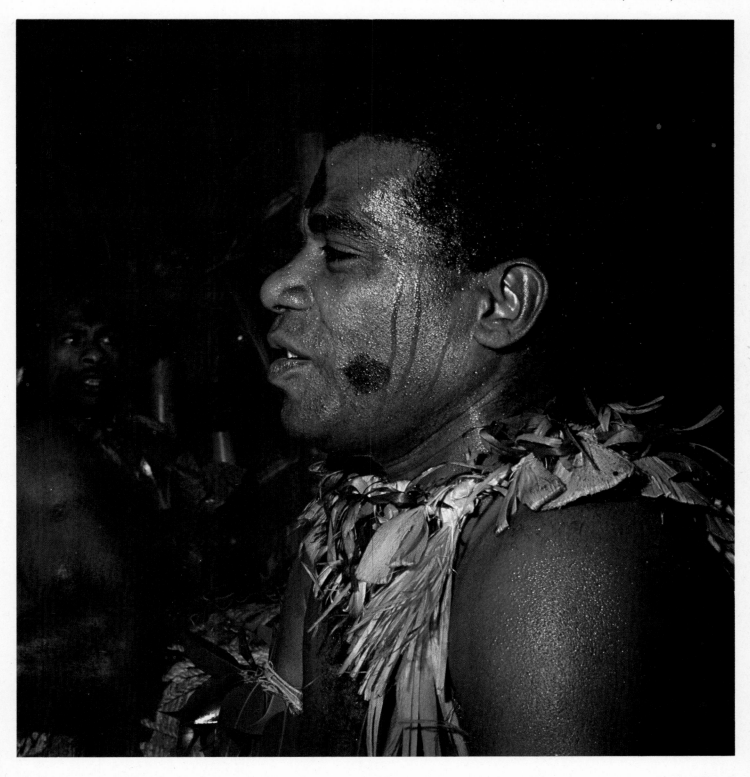

Left, interior, Viti Levu. *Lower right,* Numbutautau, central Viti Levu. The man on the left is the grandson of the chief who killed the Rev. Baker and the man with the axe that killed the Rev. Baker is the grandson of the chief who ate him. The victim in this charade is from Melbourne, Australia. Waiting for the meal is Eli Naibosi of Inland Safaris. The name of the axe is *TE VEDRIU.* If you know Fijian, you will concede it is a strange name for a battleaxe.

110

Nadrau, Viti Levu.

Left, Kerikeri, Northland. *Below*, typical farm scenes.

114

Below, Whakarewarewa thermal park, Rotorua. *Right*,
Huka Falls.

Left, artist Peter McIntyre at work at
Kakahi, central North Island, *Right,*
St Faith's Church, Rotorua and meeting
house Whakarewarewa.

Left, lake and fisherman, Karioi, Ohakune. *Right,* Taupo angler and catch. *Overleaf,* Mt Ruapehu, Tongariro National Park. *Right, top,* White Island and *below,* Ngauruhoe, New Zealand's active volcanoes.

Ninety Mile Beach, Northland

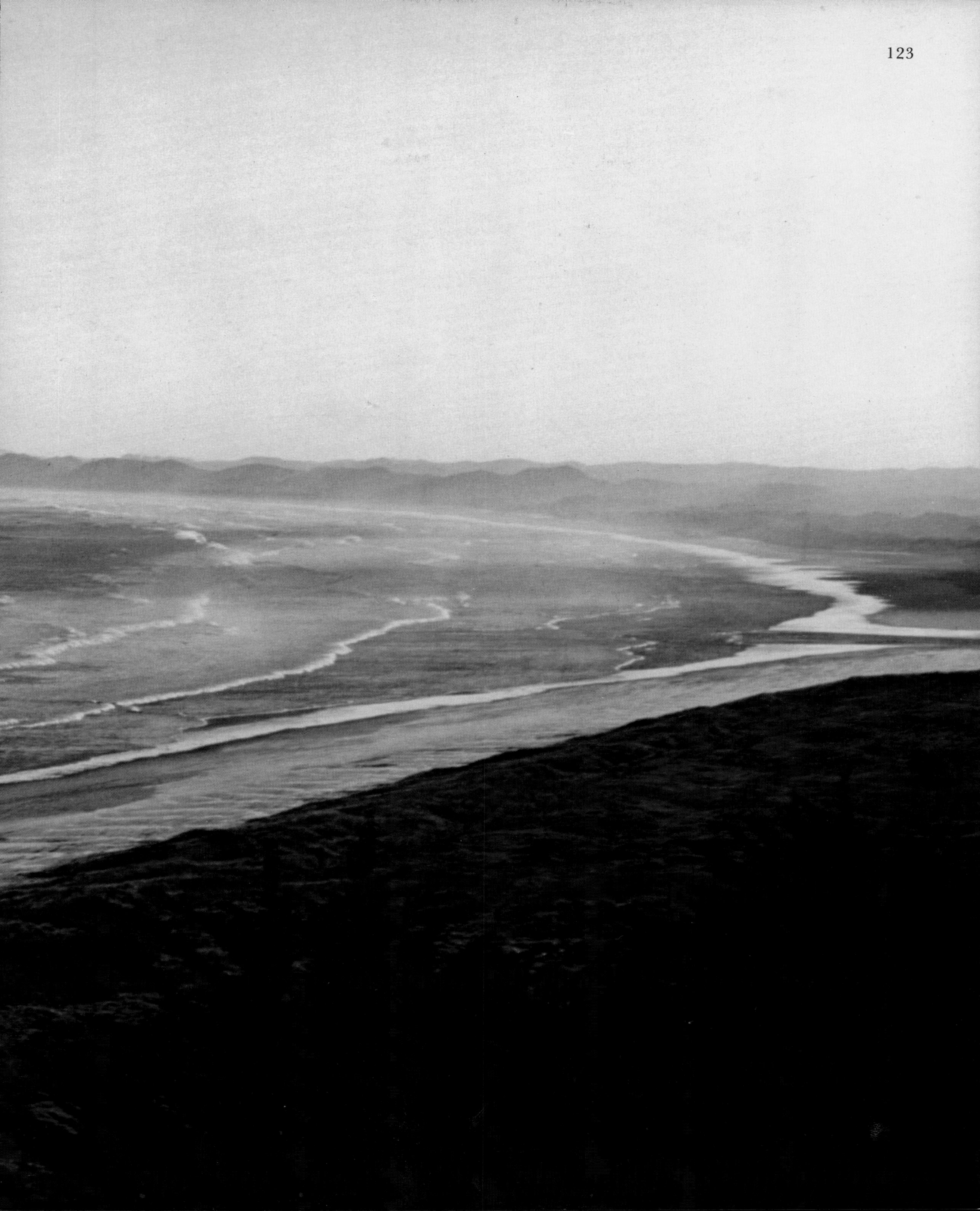

National Park. *Overleaf,*
Mt. Cook, and *opposite,*
Havelock South.

Left, Queenstown, Whakatipu. *Right,* stone cottage, Lake Hayes, Central Otago.
Overleaf, left, Mitre Peak, Milford Sound, *Right,* beech bush.

Christchurch.

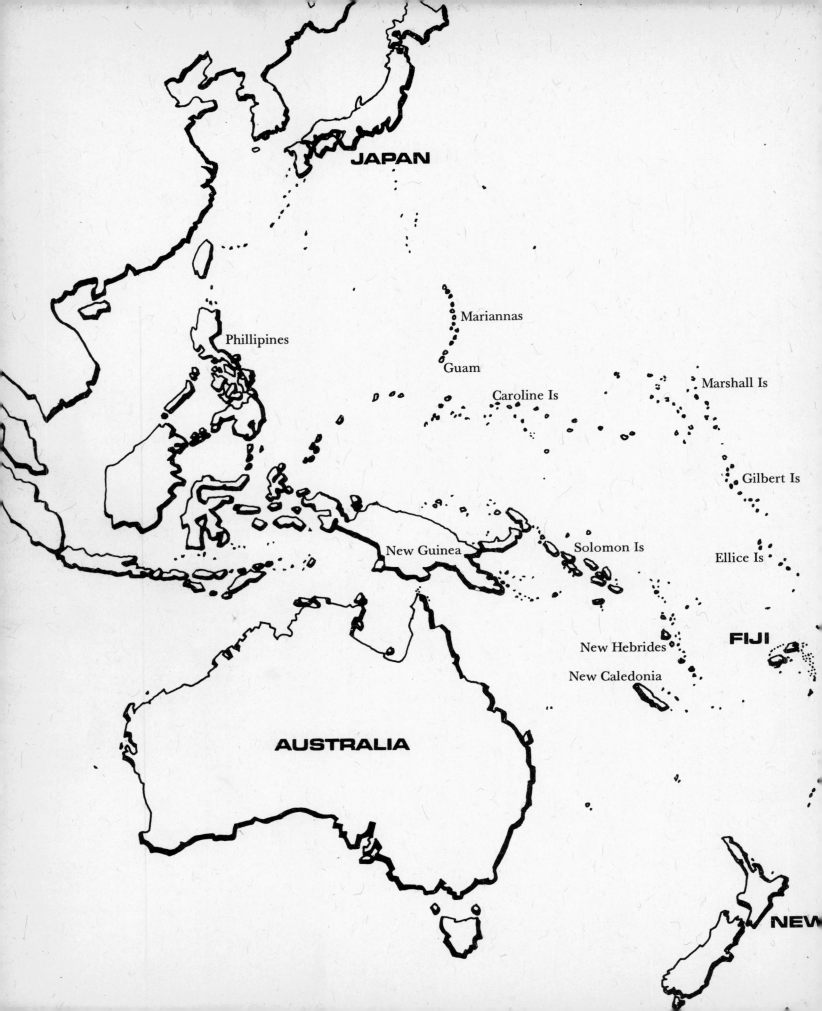